There are over 3,300 Passover Haggadah's or Seder Guides. This is a compilation of many traditional Jewish and Messianic Jewish guides. The format and flow of this booklet follows the traditional Jewish Seder order. The various blessings used in this Seder Guide are taken from the traditional Jewish and Messianic Jewish blessings. Scriptures are taken from the NIV Bible.

Passover for Christians: Complete Seder Guide & Children's Guide

By Melanie Leach & Susie Hawkins

© 2015; By Susie Hawkins and Melanie Leach. All rights reserved.

Although every precaution has been taken to verify the accuracy of the information contained herein, the authors assume no responsibility for any errors or omissions. No liability is assumed for damages that may result from the use of information contained within.

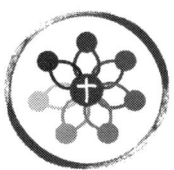

Cover Table Design by TGFX Design Studio

Cover & Back cover Layout by Happy Services via fiverr Designs

# Table of Contents

*THE COMPLETE SEDER GUIDE*     5

*THE CHILDREN'S SEDER GUIDE*     54

*ABOUT THE AUTHORS*     64

# The COMPLETE Seder Guide

INSTRUCTIONS on How To Use This Guide: This Seder Guide should be used as a tool to help inspire as well as enhance your Seder experience. By focusing and learning about Passover we see how this celebrated feast is all about Jesus, the promised Messiah.

One of the last things Jesus did on earth was celebrate a Passover meal with His disciples. It was at this meal, Jesus revealed God's overarching plan for salvation.

As you gather your group together to participate in this Passover Feast be sure everyone has a copy of this guide. You will read through this booklet rotating from person to person. Instructions are written throughout. Feel free to read those aloud or not as you go along. If you are new to this, reading aloud might be helpful.

Designate a host and hostess for your group, as each have specific tasks and help lead and guide the Seder. Keep in mind, Passover is, by tradition, an inclusive holiday and all are invited to participate – you don't have to know what to do or what comes next because the guide will walk you through it!

As you become more familiar with this tradition, you may find you want to add verses, prayers or family stories that are relevant to you and your group. We've added Notes pages throughout to help facilitate that. Make this your own!

SETTING YOUR TABLE
Items Needed for Your Seder:
- Candles (two or more)
- A platter or Seder Plate to hold the Ceremony Foods
- A Seder Guide (this book) at each place setting (people could share too)
- Matzah Cover for the Matzah (you can also use a napkin)
- Wet Wipes for the washing of hands. If you really want to do it authentically use a pitcher and basin of water for the washing of the hands

Ceremonial Foods on a Seder Plate, candles &

Ceremony Foods Needed:
- *Green herbs (parsley or lettuce)
- *Bitter herb (horseradish)
- *Haroseth (apple, honey & nut mixture)
- *Lamb shank bone
- *A dish filled with salt water for dipping
- *Boiled Egg
- Matzah (unleavened bread) covered with a napkin
- Wine or Grape Juice

* Items to be placed on a serving platter or Seder Plate.

LIGHTING OF THE CANDLES

The Hostess lights the candles to begin the Seder. While lighting the candles she prays:

HOSTESS:
Blessed are You, O Lord our God, King of the universe,
Who has sanctified us by Your commandments
And commanded us to kindle the festival lights.

Blessed are You, O Lord our God, King of the universe,
Who sanctified us with His commandments,
And commanded us to be a light to the nations
And Who gave to us Jesus our Messiah the Light of the world.

May our home be consecrated, O God,
By the Light of Your countenance,
Shining upon us in blessing and bringing us peace.

ALL: AMEN

If you prefer to say your own prayer here, that's ok. The primary purpose here is to initiate the lighting of the candles, recognizing Jesus as the Light of the world, kicking off your Passover Seder and blessing your time together.

On a large serving plate are the elements of the Seder - a dish of salt-water, horseradish, green herb (e.g. parsley), a bone from the lamb and haroset (apple, honey nut mixture). The wine and matzah are set near the Host.

[Host or Hostess explains the elements of the Seder & Seder Plate.]

NOTES:

HOST/HOSTESS: Let us review the items on the Seder Plate.

Unleavened bread, matzah: called "bread of affliction" because it recalls the unleavened bread prepared for the hasty flight by night from Egypt. The bread is broken during the Seder reminding us of Jesus's words, "this is my body."

A Green Vegetable, such as parsley: symbolizes the growth and fertility of the Jewish people in Egypt. For Christians it represents our new life and growing in our faith.

Salt Water: recalls the sweat and tears shed by the Israelite slaves and also recalls the splitting of the Red Sea as Israel passed from slavery to freedom. As Christians, we are reminded that we crossed through the waters of baptism to walk into freedom and eternal life in Jesus.

Bitter Herbs, the horseradish: Recalls the bitterness and harshness of slavery the Jews endured. As Christians, we recall the bitterness of the slavery of sin.

The Haroset, a mixture of apples, nuts, and honey: Represents the mortar the Israelites were forced to make under Pharaoh's taskmasters. The sweetness reminds them of the hope they had in freedom. For us, it reminds us that even in the toughest circumstances they are sweetened by our hope in God.

The Roasted Lamb Bone: A reminder of the Temple Sacrifice and the first Passover Lamb whose blood was put upon the doorposts of Israelites homes in Egypt. Jesus was our Passover Lamb who takes away the sins of the world once and for all.

A Roasted Egg: Serves as a symbol of life and new beginnings. As Christians, we know it's never too late for a new beginning!


THE BLESSING OF THE FEAST

HOST'S PRAYER:
Blessed are You, O Lord our God, King of the Universe,
Who has chosen us above all peoples,
And has exalted us above all tongues,
And has hallowed us with Your commandments.
In love, You have given us, O Lord our God,
Seasons for gladness, holy-days, and times for rejoicing.

This day of the feast of the unleavened bread,
The time of our freedom, an assembly day of holiness,
Is a memorial to the Exodus from Egypt. Today we also remember what Jesus did for us on the cross. He redeemed us from the slavery of sin.

You have chosen us and have sanctified us above all peoples, and You have given us Your sacred seasons for our inheritance.

Blessed are You, O Lord, Who sanctifies Israel, Brothers and Sisters in Christ and the festivals.

MIRIAM'S CUP (OPTIONAL)

(Optional: You May Choose to Skip this Section and Go To THE WASHING OF HANDS Section)

ALL ROTATE EACH PARAGRAPH:
Some Passover celebrations include a special cup called "Miriam's Cup" to honor the role of women in Jewish households and history. It is placed beside the Cup of Elijah. This is the cup of Miriam, the cup of living waters, a reminder of how God provided water in the desert during our Exodus from Egypt.

Miriam's cup is currently empty, I invite the women of at our Seder table to fill Miriam's cup with water from their own glasses.

[Pass Miriam's cup around and WOMEN fill it with water from their water glass. While the cup is being passed around the table, continue to read.]

Jewish Tradition teaches that a miraculous "well" accompanied the Hebrews throughout their journey in the desert, providing them with water. God gave this well to Miriam, to honor her bravery and devotion to the Jewish people. Miriam and her well were a spiritual oases in the desert, sources of sustenance and healing. Her words of comfort gave Hebrews faith and confidence to overcome the hardships of the Exodus.

We fill Miriam's cup with water to honor her role in ensuring the survival of the Jewish people. As keepers of traditions in the home, women passed down songs and stories, rituals and recipes, from mother to daughter, from generation to generation. As we fill the cup of Miriam with water from our own glasses, our prayer is that our daughters may continue to draw from the strength and wisdom of our heritage.

Paul mentions a "spiritual rock" that followed the Israelites in the dessert and provided water to them. He associated this "Rock" with Jesus, who is the Living Water. *"For I do not want you to be ignorant of the fact, brothers and sisters, that our ancestors were all under the cloud and that they all passed through the sea. They were all baptized into Moses in the cloud and in the sea. They all ate the same spiritual food and drank the same spiritual drink; for they drank from the spiritual rock that accompanied them, and that Rock was Christ." (I Corinthians 10:1-5)*

For Discussion (Optional): Would anyone like to share a story of a strong woman in your family and the impact she had on you? This can be a spiritual impact or a story that honors your heritage. All can participate in this.

NOTES:

_____

_____

_____

_____

_____

_____

_____

_____

THE WASHING OF HANDS – [Place wet naps or a water basin and pitcher near each place setting for the washing of hands.] You may recall in the Last Supper when Jesus washed the feet of the disciples, it was probably at this point that He did that. [Read this verse while washing hands.]

ALL WASH HANDS

PERSON TO THE LEFT OF THE HOSTESS READS, ROTATE EVERY PARAGRAPH:
"After that, he poured water into a basin and began to wash his disciples' feet, drying them with the towel that was wrapped around him... When he had finished washing their feet, he put on his clothes and returned to his place. "Do you understand what I have done for you?" he asked them. "You call me 'Teacher' and 'Lord,' and rightly so, for that is what I am. Now that I, your Lord and Teacher, have washed your feet, you also should wash one another's feet. I have set you an example that you should do as I have done for you." *(John 13:5, 12-15)*

NEXT PERSON READS:
*REVIEW THE SPECIAL ORDER OF THE SEDER* – During the Seder we drink 4 cups of wine. These cups have spiritual significance. The Seder is divided into 4 parts according to the 4 cups of wine. We drink the first two cups before the Passover Meal is served. Then the Passover meal is served and eaten. Then after the meal, two more cups are consumed to complete the Passover Seder.

The four cups represent the promises God made to the children of Israel while they were still in Egypt.

Exodus 6:5-7: "Moreover, I have heard the groaning of the

Israelites, whom the Egyptians are enslaving, and I have remembered my covenant. Therefore, say to the Israelites: 'I am the Lord, <u>and I will bring you out</u> from under the yoke of the Egyptians<u>. I will free you</u> from being slaves to them, and <u>I will redeem you</u> with an outstretched arm and with mighty acts of judgment. <u>I will take you</u> as my own people, and I will be your God. Then you will know that I am the Lord your God, who brought you out from under the yoke of the Egyptians."

The 4 Cups represent the following:
<u>Cup of Sanctification</u>: "I will bring you out." Readings are focused on God separating Israel as His chosen people. As Christians, we are called out – to be separate from the world around us.

<u>Cup of Deliverance</u>: "I will free you." During this time in the ceremony the focus is on the plagues and telling the story of Israel's deliverance. We all have a story too.

We remember and share the things He has done for us – He delivered us from the slavery of sin. After this second cup and readings, we will break for the Passover meal.

<u>Cup of Redemption</u>: "I will redeem you to myself". After the meal is finished, the third cup reminds the children of Israel that they are His chosen, redeemed people by the blood of lambs. This Cup of Redemption is where Jesus instituted the Lord's Supper. Here He instituted a new covenant. It was at this point in the Seder we are to remember His blood shed and His body broken for us when we drink the Wine and eat the Bread. He Redeemed us.

In the Old Testament Passover He saved His People, Israel.

In the Lord's Supper Jesus redeems the World once and for all in a New Covenant.

Cup of Restoration: "I will take you as my people and I will be your God." This cup looks forward to the great feast we will one day share in Heaven with Jesus. He didn't drink from this 4<sup>th</sup> cup that night. He's waiting to do that with us at the Marriage Supper of the Lamb.

As Christians we are <u>called out</u> to be separate from the world around us. Jesus <u>delivered us</u> from the slavery of sin when He <u>redeemed us</u> by dying on the cross. We now look forward to His return as King of Kings and Lord of Lords when <u>He will take us as His own and He will be our God</u> and we will dwell with Him forever.

<u>THE CUP OF SANCTIFICATION</u> – *Pour the first glass of wine.* "I will bring you out."

ALL:
Blessed are You, O Lord our God, King of the Universe, Who creates the fruit of the vine.

After this blessing, all drink the first cup.

 Father blessing his son

BLESS THE CHILDREN: If children are present, this is the time parents place their hands on each of their children's heads and bless them. Again, feel free to say your own prayer over your children. If no children present, skip to "Dip the Vegetable."

Lord, let your salvation spring up within (CHILD'S NAME), that (he/she) may obtain the salvation that is in Christ Jesus, with eternal glory. (Isaiah 45:8, 2 Timothy 2:10)

Heavenly Father, May integrity and honesty be (CHILD'S NAME) virtue and protection. (Psalm 25:21)

DIP THE VEGETABLE: [The Seder Plate is passed to all so everyone can take a piece of parsley. All dip the parsley in the salt water.]

The parsley (or green vegetable) symbolizes the growth and fertility of the Jewish people in Egypt. It also recalls their great suffering. The salt water reminds us remember the tears shed during the time of slavery in Egypt.

For Christians, it represents new life, growing in His word and discipleship in Jesus.

All take the parsley, dip it in the salt-water, and say:
Blessed are You, O Lord our God, King of the Universe, Who creates the fruit of the soil.

All eat the parsley.

THE MATZAH: The host lifts the 3 matzahs, then takes the Middle Matzah and breaks it in two. He places the larger piece back with the others (still in the middle) and wraps the smaller piece in a cloth that is hidden for the children to find. If there are no children, just set this off to the side for later use.

The Middle Matzah that is removed is called the Afikomen. We will discuss this more following the meal.

HOST: This is the bread of our affliction our fathers ate in the land of Egypt. Let all who are hungry come and eat. Let all who are in want come and celebrate the Passover with us. May it be God's will to redeem us from all evil and from all slavery.

As Believers in Christ, we too celebrate this Seder. Jesus celebrated Passover all the years of His life including the night before he died. As we participate in this Seder, consider your salvation and how the Lord, rescued you, personally, from the slavery of sin into eternal life and freedom in Jesus Christ.

NOTES:

THE 4 QUESTIONS:
"On that day tell our son, 'I do this because of what the LORD did for me when I came out of Egypt.'" (*Exodus 13:8*) The youngest child/person at the table asks the questions below.

Why is this night different from all other nights?

On all other nights we eat either leavened or unleavened bread, but on this night why only unleavened bread?

On all other nights we eat vegetables and herbs of all kinds; why on this night do we eat only bitter herbs?

On all other nights we never think of dipping herbs in water or in anything else; why on this night do we dip the parsley in salt water and the bitter herbs in haroset?

On all other nights we eat either sitting upright or reclining; why on this night do we recline as we partake of the four cups of wine?

Answering the Questions (All rotate answering the Questions): "I'm glad you've asked these questions.

Exodus 12:26-27: And when your children ask you, 'What does this ceremony mean to you?' then tell them, 'It is the Passover sacrifice to the Lord, who passed over the houses of the Israelites in Egypt and spared our homes when he struck down the Egyptians.'" Then the people bowed down and worshiped.

<u>Why do we eat only matzah?</u> When Pharaoh released our forefathers from Egypt they were forced to leave in great

haste. They had little time to bake their bread and could not wait for it to rise.

The sun beat down on the dough as they carried it along, and baked it into unleavened bread called matzah. For Christians when we share in the bread of Passover and The Lord's Supper, we share in Christ who was broken on our behalf. He is the true Bread, the Bread of Life.

<u>Why do we eat bitter herbs?</u> So that we are reminded that our forefathers were slaves in Egypt and their lives were made very bitter. We remember the bitterness of sin and our lives before Jesus.

<u>Why do we dip the herbs tonight?</u> The parsley reminds us of the hyssop used to place the blood of the lamb upon the doorposts and lintels. The salt water reminds us of the Red Sea and of the tears shed while they were in bondage. The sweet haroset reminds us that our forefathers were able to withstand bitter slavery because it was sweetened by the hope of freedom. For us, it reminds us that even in the toughest circumstances they are sweetened knowing we can trust and hope in the Lord our God.

<u>Why do we recline at the table?</u> It is because reclining was a sign of a free man long ago, and since our forefathers were freed on this night, we recline at the table. Jesus said, "Come to me, all you who are weary and burdened, and I will give you rest." Matthew 11:28

NEXT PERSON *(All rotate)*
"And you shall observe this event as an ordinance for you and your children forever." *(Exodus 12:24)*

"And when your children say to you, 'Why are we doing this?' tell them: 'It's the Passover-sacrifice to God who passed over the homes of the Israelites in Egypt when he hit Egypt with death but rescued us.'" *(Exodus 12:26-27)*

For Discussion (Optional): While Israel was in Egypt they became a great nation. They remained separated from Egypt. How has God called you to be separate from the world around you?

THE CUP OF DELIVERANCE, *The Second Cup is poured*: "I will rescue you."

All raise the second cup.
So, this promise, "I will rescue you," made to our forefathers holds true also for us.
For more than once the enemy risen up to destroy Israel and Christians. But the Lord our God, Saves us!

Put the cup down.

<u>The Plagues</u>: Here, the plagues are recited. All dip their finger in the second cup of wine or juice and recite each of the plagues while dotting the edge of each plate.

These were the ten plagues that God brought upon the Egyptians in Egypt.

Dip your finger in the wine and dot the edge of your plate while reciting the plagues.

ALL: Blood, Frogs, Gnats, Flies, Sickness, Boils, Hail, Locusts, Darkness, Death of the Firstborn. *(Your plate should have dots of wine/juice along the edge)*.

We do this because our joy is diminished due to the suffering of the Egyptian people. God has taught us to love our enemies and not to rejoice when our enemy falls. God's love is for everyone, therefore, our second cup isn't completely full because our joy is not complete.

NEXT PERSON:
Now, it is our duty from year to year to tell the story of Israel's deliverance from Egypt. The sages tell us that to dwell on it at length is accounted as praiseworthy.

We can also rejoice and keep the Passover as Christians. It reminds us of our own need for salvation. We were once slaves to sin and The Lord rescued us with a mighty hand and outstretched arm.

THE TELLING: The Story of Israel's Deliverance
(All rotate reading each paragraph)

Summarized from Genesis 47:4; Deuteronomy 10, 26; Exodus 1, 2
This is how we came to Egypt. My father and his family went down to Egypt, and lived there. We were few in number when we went, only 70 people. We moved from Canaan because there was a great famine and we needed food and pasture for our flocks. Joseph arranged with Pharaoh for us to sojourn in the land of Goshen.
While we were there we became a great nation.

We multiplied and became like the stars of heaven. We grew strong, great and powerful, and the Egyptians became afraid. They afflicted us and laid upon us hard bondage. We cried out to the Lord, the God of our fathers, and the Lord heard our voice, saw our affliction, toil and oppression, and God remembered His covenant with Abraham, Isaac and Jacob and

the Lord brought us out of Egypt with a mighty hand and outstretched arm and with great dread, and with signs, and with wonders.

Exodus 12:1-13; 28-31
GOD said to Moses and Aaron while still in Egypt, "This month is to be the first month of the year for you. Address the whole community of Israel; tell them that on the tenth of this month each man is to take a lamb for his family, one lamb to a house. If the family is too small for a lamb, then share it with a close neighbor, depending on the number of persons involved. Be mindful of how much each person will eat. Your lamb must be a healthy male, one year old; you can select it from either the sheep or the goats. Keep it penned until the fourteenth day of this month and then slaughter it—the entire community of Israel will do this—at dusk.

Then take some of the blood and smear it on the two doorposts and the lintel of the houses in which you will eat it. You are to eat the meat, roasted in the fire, that night, along with bread, made without yeast, and bitter herbs. Don't eat any of it raw or boiled in water; make sure it's roasted—the whole animal, head, legs, and innards. Don't leave any of it until morning; if there are leftovers, burn them in the fire.

And here is how you are to eat it: Be fully dressed with your sandals on and your stick in your hand. Eat in a hurry; it's the Passover to GOD.

I will go through the land of Egypt on this night and strike down every firstborn in the land of Egypt, whether human or animal, and bring judgment on all the gods of Egypt. I am GOD. The blood will serve as a sign on the houses where you live. When I see the blood I will pass over you—no disaster will touch you when I strike the land of Egypt.

The Israelites then went and did what GOD had commanded Moses and Aaron. They did it all.

At midnight GOD struck every firstborn in the land of Egypt, from the firstborn of Pharaoh, who sits on his throne, right down to the firstborn of the prisoner locked up in jail. Also the firstborn of the animals.

Pharaoh and all his servants and everyone else in Egypt got up during the night and there was loud wailing throughout Egypt. There wasn't a house in which someone wasn't dead.

Pharaoh called in Moses and Aaron that very night and said, "Get out of here - you and your Israelites! Go worship GOD on your own terms.
And yes, take your sheep and cattle as you've insisted, but go. And bless me."

ALL:
Blessed is He who keeps His promise to Israel. For the Lord premeditated the end of the bondage, fulfilling what He said to Abraham in the Covenant.

NEXT PERSON IN ROTATION: *Genesis 15:13-14*
"God said to Abram, "Know this: your descendants will live as outsiders in a land not theirs; they'll be enslaved and beaten down for 400 years. Then I'll punish their slave

masters; your offspring will march out of there loaded with plunder. But not you; you'll have a long and full life and die a good and peaceful death. Not until the fourth generation will your descendants return here."

ALL:
The Lord brought us out of Egypt.

NEXT PERSON:
"The Israelites had lived in Egypt 430 years. At the end of the 430 years, to the very day, GOD's entire army left Egypt. GOD kept watch all night, watching over the Israelites as he brought them out of Egypt.

Because GOD kept watch, all Israel for all generations will honor GOD by keeping watch this night for generations to come." *(Exodus 12:40-42)*

Exodus 13:17-22: God Leads Israel by a Pillar of Cloud by Day & Fire by Night
It so happened that after Pharaoh released the people, God didn't lead them by the road through the land of the Philistines, which was the shortest route, for God thought, "If the people encounter war, they'll change their minds and go back to Egypt." So God led the people on the wilderness road, looping around to the Red Sea. The Israelites left Egypt in military formation.

Moses took the bones of Joseph with him, for Joseph had made the Israelites solemnly swear to do it, saying, "God will surely hold you accountable, so make sure you bring my bones from here with you." They moved on from Succoth and then camped at Etham at the edge of the wilderness. God went ahead of them in a Pillar of Cloud during the day to guide them on the way, and at night in a Pillar of Fire to give them light; thus they could travel both day and night. The Pillar of Cloud by day and the Pillar of Fire by night never left the people.

Exodus 14: God Parts the Red Sea
God spoke to Moses: "Tell the Israelites to turn around and make camp at Pi Hahiroth, between Migdol and the sea. Camp on the shore of the sea opposite Baal Zephon. "Pharaoh will think, 'The Israelites are lost; they're confused. The wilderness has closed in on them.' Then I'll make Pharaoh's heart stubborn again and he'll chase after them. And I'll use Pharaoh and his army to put my Glory on display.

Then the Egyptians will realize that I am God." And that's what happened.

When the king of Egypt was told that the people were gone, he and his servants changed their minds. They said, "What have we done, letting Israel, our slave labor, go free?" So he had his chariots harnessed up and got his army together.

He took six hundred of his best chariots, with the rest of the Egyptian chariots and their drivers coming along.

God made Pharaoh king of Egypt stubborn, determined to chase the Israelites as they walked out on him without even looking back. The Egyptians gave chase and caught up with them where they had made camp by the sea—all Pharaoh's horse-drawn chariots and their riders, all his foot soldiers there at Pi Hahiroth opposite Baal Zephon.

As Pharaoh approached, the Israelites looked up and saw them— Egyptians! Coming at them! They were terrified and cried out to the Lord. They told Moses, "Weren't the cemeteries large enough in Egypt so that you had to take us out here in the wilderness to die? What have you done to us, taking us out of Egypt? Back in Egypt didn't we tell you this would happen? Didn't we tell you,

'Leave us alone here in Egypt - we're better off as slaves in Egypt than as corpses in the wilderness.'"

Moses spoke to the people: "Don't be afraid. Stand firm and watch God do his work of salvation for you today. Take a good look at the Egyptians today for you're never going to see them again. God will fight the battle for you. You need only to be still!"

…The angel of God that had been leading the camp of Israel now shifted and got behind them. And the Pillar of Cloud that had been in front also shifted to the rear. The Cloud was now between the camp of Egypt and the camp of Israel. The Cloud enshrouded one camp in darkness and flooded the other with light. The two camps didn't come near each other all night.

Then Moses stretched out his hand over the sea and God, with a terrific east wind all night long, made the sea go back. He made the sea dry ground. The seawaters split.

The Israelites walked through the sea on dry ground with the waters a wall to the right and to the left. The Egyptians came after them in full pursuit, every horse and chariot and driver of Pharaoh racing into the middle of the sea. It was now the morning watch. God looked down from the Pillar of Fire and Cloud on the Egyptian army and threw them into a panic. He clogged the wheels of their chariots; they were stuck in the mud. The Egyptians said, "Run from Israel! God is fighting on their side and against Egypt!"

God said to Moses, "Stretch out your hand over the sea and the waters will come back over the Egyptians, over their chariots, over their horsemen." Moses stretched his hand out over the sea: As the day broke and the Egyptians were running, the sea returned to its place as before. God dumped the Egyptians in the middle of the sea. The waters returned, drowning the chariots and riders of Pharaoh's army that had chased after Israel into the sea. Not one of them survived.

But the Israelites walked right through the middle of the sea on dry ground, the waters forming a wall to the right and to the left. God delivered Israel that day from the oppression of the Egyptians. And Israel looked at the Egyptian dead, washed up on the shore of the sea, and realized the tremendous power that God brought against the Egyptians. The people were in reverent awe before God and trusted in God and his servant Moses.

After witnessing this great miracle, Moses and the people sang a song of praise to God for their deliverance, and Miriam led the women in a joyous dance…

And so began Israel's journey from slavery to freedom, from sadness to joy, from being strangers in Egypt to becoming a great nation. The crossing of the sea represented the birth of a new nation, redeemed by the blood of lambs.

Moses told the people, "Remember the day which you came out from Egypt, out of the house of slavery, for by a strong hand the Lord brought you out of that place.
You shall tell your son on that day, 'It is because of what the Lord did for me when I came out of Egypt.'

You shall therefore keep this statue at its appointed time from year to year. Now let us all say:

ALL:
Amen

"Telling the Story" of Deliverance

NOTES:

PRAISE GOD: "DAYENU"

In light of all that God has done for us, we surely should express our heartfelt gratitude and give thanks for our salvation. It is customary to sing some verses of the ancient Hebrew song Dayenu (DI – AYE – NUE) which means "it would have been enough for us"):

Many Jewish families sing this in Hebrew. We will read it in English, you can also download it and sing along. It's a catchy tune!

NEXT PERSON IN ROTATION BEGINS: You can find the song, "Dayeinu" (pronounced, dah-YAY-noo) on iTunes.

Had He brought us out from Egypt and not executed judgment against them, DAYEINU!
Had He executed judgment against them and not done justice to their idols, DAYEINU!
Had He done justice to their idols and not slain their first-born DAYEINU!
Had He slain their first-born and not given us their property DAYEINU!
Had He given us their property, and not divided the sea for us DAYEINU!
It would have been enough for us "if through Jesus, we received eternal salvation and not received His Holy Spirit. DAYEINU!
Had He given us His Holy Spirit and not bestowed us with the fruit of the Spirit. It would have been enough for us. DAYEINU!
Had He bestowed us with the fruit of the Spirit and not given us His peace. It would have been enough for us. DAYEINU!

[In the Jewish Seder Guide there are 26 verses to this song. I say DAYEINU at eight!]

ALL:
Dayeinu! Amen!

The Host holds up or points to the shank bone on the Seder Plate, then reads:

The Passover Sacrifice, the lamb, which our fathers used to eat at the time when the temple still stood – what was the reason for it?

NEXT PERSON IN ROTATION:
Because the Lord, passed over the houses of our Fathers in Egypt. As it is said, It is the sacrifice of the Lord's Passover, for He passed over the homes of the Children of Israel, when he struck the Egyptians; He passed over our homes and did not come in to destroy us.

The children of Israel were told how to protect themselves from the last plague – the plague of death. Each family was to take a lamb, kill it and drain the blood into a basin; and then take hyssop and dip it in the blood and apply the blood to their doorposts – along the top and sides.

During this part of the Seder you can have the children or your group place red streamers around the doorposts as a visual to remember year after year.

As believers we know Jesus shed His blood as a final sacrifice for us. John the Baptist said, "Behold the Lamb of God who takes away the sins of the world!" (John 1:29)

 Red streamers placed on the front door

Jewish Believers say the Passover Feast was an enactment or a rehearsal each year so the Jewish people would know and recognize the Messiah when He came. Passover pointed to Jesus.

In Exodus 12, we read what was to happen in Jerusalem on Passover. On the 10th of Nisan, the Passover Lamb was led through the Sheep Gate for its journey to the temple. The lamb was then taken to the temple where it was kept four days under close observation. (Ex 12:3&6) According to Jewish tradition there were several tests performed on the lambs to ensure it's purity.

On the 14th day, after it was declared pure, it was placed on the altar to remain there until 3p.m. for the sacrifice. Not one bone was to be broken.

The similarities between the Passover Lamb and Jesus, the Lamb of God, are hard to miss! Jesus entered Jerusalem on Palm Sunday, the 10th of Nisan (4 days before Passover). He was closely watched and questioned by the religious leaders during those four days. The priests tried to trap him that week while He taught in the temple, but they couldn't do it.

They arrested him in the night and early Friday morning, Pilate declared Him INNOCENT – PURE.

Jesus had done NOTHING deserving of death.

On Good Friday, because it was almost sundown – and Jewish Sabbath begins at sundown - they broke the legs of the other criminals on the cross but not Jesus's legs, because at 3p.m. – the same time of the Passover sacrifice - He gave up the ghost and died.

This is the story Jewish Believers and Christians tell at Passover. Jesus is the Passover Lamb, who takes away the sins of the world.

"The blood will serve as a sign on the houses where you live. When I see the blood I will pass over you - no disaster will touch you when I strike the land of Egypt." *(Exodus 12:13)*

But why did the children of Israel need to be protected against the angel of death who was sent out to execute judgment on the Egyptians? This is the only plague that required Israel to do something. The answer is found throughout the Bible, "Indeed, there is no one on earth who is righteous, no one who does what is right and never sins." *(Ecclesiastes 7:20)*. "The one who sins is the one who will die." *(Ezekiel 18:20)*.

Everyone who fails to live up to the moral law of God is guilty and has to pay with his or her life. In the Old Testament Law, the blood of an unblemished lamb became the symbol of an innocent life covering the guilty life from the eyes of a Holy and just God.

"When I see the blood I will pass over you."

The prophet Isaiah wrote about the Messiah when he said, "We all, like sheep, have gone astray, each of us has turned to our own way; and the Lord has laid ON HIM the iniquity of us all. He was oppressed and afflicted, yet he did not open his mouth; he was led like a lamb to the slaughter and as a sheep before its shearers is silent, so he did not open his mouth." *(Isaiah 53:5-7)*

John, the Baptist, seeing Jesus said, "Behold, the Lamb of God who takes away the sins of the world." *(John 1:29)*

I Corinthians 5:7 says, "For Christ, our Passover lamb, has been sacrificed." God transferred our sin to the sinless Christ Jesus. By believing and trusting in Him, we are forgiven and saved! In Him Passover is fulfilled and salvation has come to The World.

NOTES:

The Host lifts his cup of wine and says…

HOST:
Therefore, it is our duty to thank, praise, glorify, extol, bless, exalt and adore Him Who did all of these miracles for our fathers and for us. He has brought us from slavery to freedom, from sorrow to joy, from mourning to festive days, from darkness to a great light, and from subjection to redemption.

Let us then recite before Him a new song.

Host sets down his cup of wine without drinking it.

ALL STAND and recite Psalm 114, continue rotating individual readings.

ALL:
HALLELUJAH, praise the Lord!

READING:
After Israel left Egypt, The house of Jacob left those barbarians behind;

ALL:
All Judea was made his sanctuary: Israel his dominion.

READING:
The sea looked and fled: The Jordan river was turned back.

ALL:
The mountains skipped like rams: And the hills like the lambs of the flock.

READING:
What ailed you, O sea, that you turned and ran away:
And you, O Jordan, that you were turned back?

ALL:
You mountains, that you skipped like rams:
And you hills like lambs of the flock?

READING:
At the presence of the Lord the earth was moved:
At the presence of the God of Jacob:

ALL:
He turned the rock into pools of water:
And the stony hill into fountains of waters.
HALLELUJAH, Praise the Lord!

All are seated.

THE BLESSING OF THE CEREMONIAL FOOD

The HOST takes the cup in his hand and says:

Blessed are You, O Lord our God, King of the Universe, Who has redeemed us and our fathers from Egypt, and has permitted us to live until this night, to partake of the unleavened bread and the bitter herbs.

HOSTESS:
Blessed are you, O God, for you have, in mercy supplied all our needs. You have given us Jesus, forgiveness for sin, life abundant and life everlasting. Hallelujah!

ALL:
Blessed are You, O Lord our God, King of the universe, Who creates the fruit of the vine.

One of the key customs at Passover is to relate personally to the story as though you, yourself came up out of Egypt. As Christians, we can relate – we were slaves to our sins and in Jesus we are set FREE! As we drink the second cup, we thank God for delivering us with His mighty hand!

All drink the second cup of wine, The Cup of Deliverance.

With the final plague – the death of the firstborn, Israel was free! With Jesus's death on the cross, we are free.
For Discussion (Optional): How has Jesus set you free? What's your story? Have you or your family experienced miracles or something you knew was God working and moving in your life? Those who want to share, may do so here.

Now, the leader lifts up the stack of matzah.

HOST: Blessed are You, O Lord our God, King of the Universe, Who brings forth bread from the earth.

Now, the Host takes the bottom matzah and passes it to all at the table. Each person should break off <u>FIVE</u> olive size pieces.

Once everyone has gotten their 5 pieces of bread, hold one piece up and ALL say:

Blessed are You, O Lord our God, King of the Universe, Who has sanctified us by Your commandments and has commanded us to eat the unleavened bread.

The unleavened bread, the bread of affliction represents Jesus. It is made of only flour and water – no yeast – a symbol of sin. After the dough is flattened, before baking, it is pierced and striped with a pointed tool to keep it from bubbling during the cooking process.

Jesus was sinless – pure. His hands and feet were pierced with nails on the cross. His side pierced with the spear.

"But he was pierced for our transgressions, he was crushed for our sins; the punishment that brought us peace was on him, and by his wounds we are healed." *(Isaiah 53:5)*

All eat the bread.

Participant eating the bitter herb (horseradish).

We eat bitter herbs to recall that the Egyptians embittered the lives of our fathers, as it is written: "And the Egyptians hated the children of Israel, and afflicted them and mocked them: And they made their life bitter with hard works in clay, and brick, and with all manner of service wherewith they were overcharged in the works of the earth." *(Exodus 1:13-14)* When we eat the bitter herbs, we remember the sorrow, persecution, and suffering of our life in bondage.

As the bitter herbs bring tears to our eyes, so we remember the affliction of our people.

As Christians, eating the bitter herbs reminds us of our lives before we knew Jesus as Savior. The bitter herbs represent the bitter cup our Lord tasted on our behalf. The horseradish brings tears to our eyes as we taste it and remember.

ALL:
Blessed are You, O Lord our God, King of the Universe, Who has sanctified us by Your commandments and has commanded us concerning the eating of bitter herbs.

Dip one piece of matzah in the horseradish. All eat the bread and horseradish together.

The Haroset represents the mortar the Israelites were forced to make under Pharaoh's taskmasters. The sweetness reminds us of the hope they had in freedom. For us, it reminds us that even in the toughest circumstances they are sweetened by our hope in God.

Dip the third piece of matzah in the haroset. All eat the bread and haroset.

READING:
In the days of the Second Temple, an argument broke out among the sages. The sage Hillel thought the matzah and bitter herbs should be eaten together; however, other sages thought they should be eaten separately.

Therefore, the tradition began to do it both ways – we first eat the bitter herbs separately, then together with the Hillel Sandwich.

Now, place horseradish and haroset between two pieces of unleavened bread (The Hillel Sandwich).

All eat the Hillel sandwich.
This concludes the Ceremonial Meal.

THE PASSOVER SUPPER is now served. Set aside your Seder Guides and enjoy the meal. Host blesses the meal and the time together. Your key goal here is to spend time together focused on the true meaning of Easter – Jesus came and became our Passover Lamb.

HOST BLESSES THE MEAL:
Blessed are You, O Lord our God, King of the Universe, Who has sanctified us with His commandments, and commanded us to eat the Passover Meal.


[AFTER THE MEAL]
THE CUP OF REDEMPTION, The Third Cup is Poured: "I will redeem you"

By this time in the meal, the lost Afikomen should have been found and a reward given by the Host.

The host unwraps the Afikomen and breaks it into small pieces and distributes it to all present.

NEXT PERSON IN THE ROTATION:
It is customary to end the Passover meal by eating this final piece of unleavened bread that was 'lost' – the Afikoman. The word "Afikoman" is Greek and means "the coming one."

This is the broken piece of matzah that was hidden away earlier this evening. When this middle piece was broken at the start of our Seder, it symbolized the breaking of the body of the Son of God. This half was separated and wrapped in linen, foreshadowing the wrapping of Christ's body after the crucifixion. When the broken and wrapped bread was hidden, this symbolized Jesus's burial. When the Afikomen is found and redeemed, this represents His resurrection.

For it is written, "During the meal, Jesus took and blessed the bread, broke it, and gave it to His disciples: Take, eat. This is my body." *(Matthew 26:26)*

The Bible also says, "Let me go over with you again exactly what goes on in the Lord's Supper and why it is so centrally important. I received my instructions from the Master himself and passed them on to you. The Master, Jesus, on the night of his betrayal, took bread. Having given thanks, he broke it and said, this is my body, broken for you. Do this to remember me." *(I Corinthians 11:23-24)*

All hold the bread.

HOST:
This broken bread represents Jesus, the Messiah's body that was broken for you on the cross.

Blessed are you, LORD our God, King of the universe, Who brings forth bread from the earth.

NOTES:

HOSTESS:
Jesus also said, "I am the bread of life." *(John 6:48)* and "I am the living bread that came down from heaven. Whoever eats this bread will live forever. This bread is my flesh, which I will give for the life of the world." *(John 6:51)*

We pause in silence and consider the bread in our hands and what it represents. Leaven is a symbol of sin, and Jesus was sinless. This represents the sinless body of Christ broken for us.

HOST:
The Afikoman memorializes Jesus's sacrifice of atonement for our sins so that we might have peace with God. We remember what He did because He loves us.

(OPTIONAL CONTEMPLATION AND READINGS) When we eat the broken matzah, we remember is suffering. Jesus in the Garden (Matthew 26:36-46), Jesus on Trial (Matthew 26:57-75), Jesus Wears the Crown of Thorns (Matthew 27:26-31), Jesus on His Way to the Cross (Luke 23:26-32), Jesus Dies on the Cross (Mark 15:1-47) and Jesus Laid in the Tomb (Luke 23:50-56).

We will add the additional blessing, thanking the LORD God of Israel for providing us with the true Bread from Heaven, His beloved Son: Blessed are You, LORD our God, King of the universe, who brings forth the True Bread from Heaven. Let us bless the Lord.

If you have believers at your table, you may conduct The Lord's Supper here. If there are non-believers, you can just continue and not call it The Lord's Super.

NOTES:

All eat the bread. The Third cup of wine is poured now.

HOST:
Then he took the Third Cup of Wine – the Cup of Redemption.

I will Redeem you with an outstretched arm. (Exodus 6:6)

Surely, the arm of the Lord is not too short to save. (Isaiah 59:1)

It is our own righteousness that that falls short. Therefore, His own arm brought him salvation, and his own righteousness sustained him. (Isaiah 59:16)

Matthew 26:27-29: Then he took a cup, and when he had given thanks, he gave it to them, saying, "Drink from it, all of you. This is my blood of the covenant, which is poured out for many for the forgiveness of sins. I tell you, I will not drink from this fruit of the vine from now on until that day when I drink it new with you in my Father's kingdom."

Just as the blood of the lamb brought salvation in Egypt, so Jesus's atoning death brings salvation to all who believe.

Blessed are you, O Lord our God, ruler of the universe, who creates the fruit of the vine. Let us gratefully drink.

All drink the third cup of Redemption.

For Discussion (Optional): Consider The Lord's Supper, what are your thoughts as you eat the bread and drink the wine/juice?

The Fourth Cup: The Cup of Restoration: I will take you as MY people and I will be your God.

The fourth cup is filled.

Psalm 118
Give thanks to the Lord, for he is good; His love endures forever.

Let Israel say: "His love endures forever." Let the house of Aaron say: "His love endures forever." Let those who fear the Lord say: "His love endures forever."

When hard pressed, I cried to the Lord; he brought me into a spacious place. The Lord is with me; I will not be afraid. What can mere mortals do to me?
The Lord is with me; he is my helper. I look in triumph on my enemies.

It is better to take refuge in the Lord than to trust in humans. It is better to take refuge in the Lord than to trust in princes. All the nations surrounded me, but in the name of the Lord I cut them down. They surrounded me on every side, but in the name of the Lord I cut them down.

They swarmed around me like bees, but they were consumed as quickly as burning thorns; in the name of the Lord I cut them down. I was pushed back and about to fall, but the Lord helped me. The Lord is my strength and my defense; he has become my salvation.

Shouts of joy and victory resound in the tents of the righteous: "The Lord's right hand has done mighty things! The Lord's right hand is lifted high; the Lord's right hand has done mighty things!" I will not die but live, and will proclaim what the Lord has done. The Lord has chastened me severely, but he has not given me over to death. Open for me the gates of the righteous; I will enter and give thanks to the Lord. This is the gate of the Lord through which the righteous may enter. I will give you thanks, for you answered me; you have become my salvation.

The stone the builders rejected has become the cornerstone; the Lord has done this, and it is marvelous in our eyes. The Lord has done it this very day; let us rejoice today and be glad.

Lord, save us! Lord, grant us success! Blessed is he who comes in the name of the Lord. From the house of the Lord we bless you. The Lord is God, and he has made his light shine on us. With boughs in hand, join in the festal procession up to the horns of the altar.

You are my God, and I will praise you; you are my God, and I will exalt you.

Give thanks to the Lord, for he is good; his love endures forever! Let everything that has breath Praise the Lord! *(Psalm 150:6)*

THE CUP OF ELIJAH: Have the children open the front door.

HOSTESS:
Tradition holds that we save an extra place for Elijah. The door is open for Elijah to arrive and announce that the Messiah has come. Jesus spoke of John the Baptist as His forerunner saying:

*(Mark 9:11-13; Matthew 11:13-15)* And they asked him (Jesus), "Why do the teachers of the law say that Elijah must come first?" Jesus replied, "To be sure, Elijah does come first, and restores all things. Why then is it written that the Son of Man must suffer much and be rejected? But I tell you, Elijah has come, and they have done to him everything they wished, just as it is written about him." For all the Prophets and the Law prophesied until John. And if you are willing to accept it, he is the Elijah who was to come.
He who has ears, let him hear.

NOTES:

_____

_____

_____

_____

_____

_____

_____

_____

_____

"Elijah has come" This was true in the person of John the Baptist.

So please close the door and be seated. Elijah and the Messiah have already come and we now await His triumphant return as King of Kings and Lord of Lords!

During the Last Supper, Jesus did not drink the fourth cup (the cup of Restoration), but promised to do so with His disciples in the Kingdom to come. This cup looks forward to the day when Jesus comes back for His bride, the church for the Wedding Supper of the Lamb.

Revelation 19:6-9, excerpts: "Then I heard what sounded like a great multitude… shouting: "Hallelujah! For our Lord God Almighty reigns. Let us rejoice and be glad… For the wedding of the lamb has come, and his bride has made herself ready"… Then the angel said to me, "Write this: Blessed are those who are invited to the wedding supper of the Lamb!""

The Passover is central to the overarching story of God's Redemptive Plan for the world. It begins with Passover where He saved His people Israel, it moves to the Lord's Supper where Christ redeems sinners.

Currently, we are between Feasts – the Lord's Supper and the Wedding Supper of the Lamb.

Revelations 21:1-4, excerpts: Then I saw a new Heaven and a new earth, for the first heaven and the first earth had passed away… I saw the Holy City, the New Jerusalem, coming down out of heaven from God… And I heard a loud voice from the throne saying, "Look! God's dwelling place is now among the people, and He will dwell with them. They will be His people, and God Himself will be with them and be their God."

The 4th Cup, The Cup of Restoration - "I will take you as my people and I will be your God."

This cup looks forward to the day when Jesus comes back to take us to be with Him and to restore His Kingdom.

All raise their cups and say:

We Praise You, O Lord our God, King of the Universe, Who has created the fruit of the vine.

All drink the fourth cup.

HOST: Our Passover Seder is now complete. Lord, grant us peace that we may do your will.

The Host says a final blessing:
The Lord bless you and keep you, The Lord make his face shine upon you and be gracious to you, The Lord turn his face toward you and give you peace!
Amen!

ALL: Next Year, In Jerusalem!

This concludes the Passover Seder.

# The Children's Seder Guide

This Seder is designed for children under twelve. Since the Passover Seder is a multi-sensory experience, feel free to experiment with the foods, the Seder order and the way you tell the story. We have included supplementary suggestions for making this meaningful and enjoyable for kids (and therefore their parents!) If you have children who read, they can participate in reading the Exodus story and the questions and answers. It's helpful to read the story out of a children's Bible or storybook, since it is usually more concise, or print off scripture passages in a contemporary translation.

Many families have used this Children's Seder Outline to create their own Family Seder. It provides a great framework for you and your family to build upon, if you so desire.

Lighting of the Candles:  The hostess/mother lights two white tapered candles; she prays for the Spirit of God to bless her family and be with them as they observe this Passover Seder.

Blessing the Children: The host/father stands with the children and prays individually over each one, asking God's blessing on them.

The traditional prayer is from Numbers 6:24-26 "The Lord bless you and keep you; the Lord make his face shine on you and be gracious to you, the Lord turn his face toward you and give you peace."

Story of the Passover: Read Exodus 12 (if you have readers, divide up the story into segments each can read). Or, read the story and have children re-tell it. You may also have the children re-inact the story by dressing up and putting on a play.

The Afikomen: The host/father shows the children the three matzah crackers wrapped in cloth. He explains the matzah, the unleavened bread that the Israelites ate as they left Egypt.  He breaks the middle matzah in half; wraps one half in another cloth that someone hides in the next room, the other half returns to the matzah bag.

The Four Questions:
Host/Father reads: "And when your children ask you, 'What does this ceremony mean to you?' then tell them,

'It is the Passover sacrifice to the Lord, who passed over the houses of the Israelites in Egypt and spared our homes when he struck down the Egyptians" (Ex. 12:26-27.)

NOTES:

Children ask the following questions: Reader 1:
Question: Why on all other nights do we eat leavened bread, but on this night only unleavened?

Answer: When Pharaoh agreed to let the Israelites leave Egypt, they had to leave in a big hurry! They didn't have time for their bread to "rise" (explain.)

Reader 2:
Question: Why on all other nights do we eat all kinds of vegetables but on this night only bitter ones?

Answer: The bad taste reminds us of how bad it felt to be slaves and how bad it feels to disobey God.

Reader 3:
Question: Why on all other nights do we not dip our foods even once, but on this night we dip twice?

Answer: The parsley dipped in salt water reminds us of the branches used to put the lamb's blood over the door and the tears the Israelites cried as the prayed to God for deliverance. The sweet haroset reminds us of the freedom that God gave His people and the sweetness of hope and happiness.

Reader 4:
Question: Why on all other nights do we eat sitting, but tonight we recline?

Answer: We are safe and do not have to leave our homes in a hurry to escape Pharaoh like the Israelites did. God has blessed us; we can relax and be safe in our homes as we eat this meal.

Pass the Seder plate: Each person takes a small portion. Explain the meaning of the foods and have everyone taste at the same time.

Matzah – a flat bread, an unleavened cracker, the bread the Israelites ate

Grape Juice – represents blood (the Nile turning to blood) and all the plagues. Have children dip little finger in juice and put a dot on the edge of their plate for each plague: blood, frogs, gnats, flies, sickness, boils, hail, locusts, darkness, death of firstborn.

Bitter Herb – represents the tears of slavery

Explain the food on the Seder Plate:
Parsley – represents new life, hope

Salt Water – represents the Red Sea, which the Israelites would miraculously cross

Haroset (apple mixture) – the sweetness reminds them of the hope Israel had in God to deliver them from slavery

Egg – represents new life (the egg isn't in the biblical story, but is traditional in Jewish homes)

Lamb bone – represents the Passover Lamb

Optional Plague Activity: In many Jewish homes the children have activities for each of the 10 plagues. If you are also conducting a Seder for the Adults this is a good way to include children before they retire for bed.

| Plague | Activity(ies) |
| --- | --- |
| Nile turns to blood | Take bottled water and have children drop red food coloring it |
| Frogs | In some Jewish stores, they sell chocolate frogs. Pass these out to the children and adults as a sweet treat |
| Gnats & Flies | Have the children grind up pepper on their plates to represent gnats and flies |
| Sickness | They can draw a picture or walk around the table like they are sick. This usually looks like a zombie-walk |
| Boils | Use red dot stickers and the kids can stick them on themselves and each other |
| Hail | Indoor firecrackers are fun for this, but kind of messy. There are also bounce balls they can bounce around. |
| Locusts | The Jewish Bag of Plagues has a good locust in there that we use. If you have toy bugs, those will do fine as well. |
| Darkness | Blindfold the children and have them lead one another around the table. You can also turn off the lights for a time. |
| Death of the Firstborn | Use red streamers and tape the "blood of the lamb" over your door and lintels to demonstrate what Israel did to be saved from the final plague. |

There are Jewish Stores online where you can find "Bags of Plagues." These are fun for the children too.

NOTES:

The Lord's Supper:  Explain that the night before Jesus' death, He celebrated the Passover with His disciples; eating the same kind of foods the children just ate. At that Seder, Jesus began the Lord's Supper (Communion), which was taking the matzah and juice of the Seder and giving it additional meaning. The bread represents His body and the juice, His blood, given on the cross for us.

Reader: Read Luke 22:15-20 (depending on readers' age, it is helpful to print out children's translation for them). Emphasize that we "do this" to remember Jesus' death.

The Afikomen: Remember the half of the matzah that was hidden? Now children go into the next room to look for it. The winner receives a small prize, a piece of candy or $1. There is frequently some bargaining, the children asking for a little more than the host was planning!

Conclusion: The Passover is the story of not only Moses and the Israelites, but also of Jesus. We remember his suffering on the cross and that even though we are sinners; Jesus loves us so much that He gave His life for us.  We are thankful!

Sing a praise song that children know, one that they choose. This is how Jesus and disciples concluded their Passover, "When they had sung a hymn, they went out…"

For more information on the Passover Seder, what it is, why Christians should better understand it and how to celebrate it; our book "Passover for Christians" is available at Amazon.com. You can also visit www.passoverforchristians.com to find other resources and information.

# About the Authors

Melanie Leach lives in Dallas, Texas. She graduated from Nicholls State University and has worked in marketing for the past twenty years. She and her husband, Will, have led Christian Passover Seders many years in their home. Her hope is to introduce this beautiful Jewish tradition to Christians and create meaningful, rich traditions in homes everywhere. Melanie also enjoys cooking, playing tennis, traveling with her husband and keeping up with their six year old son, Nicholas.

Susie Hawkins lives in Dallas and has been actively involved in ministry as a pastor's wife, teacher and volunteer. She enjoys traveling to Israel with her husband O.S. and has been exploring Christianity's Jewish roots and its rich history these past thirty years. She has participated in Seders while in Florida, Texas and Israel and wants others to share in these valuable insights and discoveries. Susie and OS have two married daughters and six young grandchildren who have served as her guinea pigs in exploring with others why Passover is "a night that is different from any other night."

Made in the USA
San Bernardino, CA
25 April 2016